Eleanor, Speak

poems by

Nan Ottenritter

Finishing Line Press
Georgetown, Kentucky

Eleanor, Speak

Copyright © 2021 by Nan Ottenritter
ISBN 978-1-64662-517-8 First Edition
All rights reserved under International and Pan-American Copyright Conventions.
No part of this book may be reproduced in any manner whatsoever without written permission from the publisher, except in the case of brief quotations embodied in critical articles and reviews.

ACKNOWLEDGMENTS

I thank the following journals (and their editors) in which these poems have appeared:

Artemis: "Verdi Would Have Wept" and "Eleanor, Speak"
TheNewVerse.News: "Making of an Enemy"
Anthology of the Poetry Society of Virginia: "Little Lincoln"
Poets Reading the News: "Keeping Count"
As You Were: The Military Review: "Metallic Transfer Cases"

Thanks to the women who have inspired these poems. Named and unnamed, real or imagined, you are a stunning lot.

Thanks to my poetry friends and teachers: Leslie, David, Doug, Rose, Joanna, Cathryn, Wendy, Marsha, Guy, Jenny, Julie, Karen, Molly, Stella, ModPo, Mme. Conrad, and all of the poets I have heard and read.

Thanks to both the written and spoken word. What an exquisite puzzle it is to translate life into symbol and sound.

Publisher: Leah Huete de Maines
FLP Editor: Christen Kincaid
Copyeditor: Gail Robinson
Author Photo: Melissa Rayford
Cover Design: Elizabeth Maines McCleavy and Nan Ottenritter
Cover Photos:
    Upper row, left: Florence Foster Jenkins, unknown author/public domain
    Upper row, center: Mourner, Louvre Museum/public domain
    Upper row, right: Eleanor Roosevelt, Douglas Chandor, White House/public domain
    Middle row, left: Agatha Christie, Violetriya/CC BY-SA 3.0
    Middle row, right: Camille Claudel, Plombelec/CC BY-SA 4.0
    Bottom row, left: Queen Elizabeth, Associated Press/public domain
    Bottom row, center: Notre-Dame de Paris, Peter Haas/CC BY-SA 3.0
    Bottom row, right: Emma Ottenritter, unknown author/family photo

Order online: www.finishinglinepress.com
        also available on amazon.com

Author inquiries and mail orders:
Finishing Line Press
PO Box 1626
Georgetown, Kentucky 40324
USA

Table of Contents

The Seventy-Third Book: Letter to Agatha Christie 1

Verdi Would Have Wept 2

mom's cast-iron skillet 4

Family Traumas 5

It's Time for a Cat 6

Educating Rachael 7

Little Lincoln 8

after dessert 9

When My Mother Met the Queen 10

Four Poems on Camille Claudel

    The Devil's Basket 12

    Too Many Ideas 13

    Camille Bicycles through Paris, Spring 1887 14

    I Take My Hammer 16

I Know How 17

Keeping Count 18

Making of an Enemy 20

Metallic Transfer Cases 21

The End of This 22

Downsizing 23

The Gesture 24

Bus Stop to Nowhere 25

Eleanor, Speak 26

Notre Dame 27

Notes 28

for my parents and teachers

The Seventy-Third Book: Letter to Agatha Christie

Dear Agatha, I start with a confession: I don't remember
ever having read any of your creations. I don't

like mysteries and, even at my best, lack some critical
neuron that keeps all those facts firing in my brain.

Sixty-six novels, fourteen short story collections, the longest-running
play in the world. Over four billion books published—

first the Bible, then Shakespeare, then you!
I sit in awe at this latest development,

Alzheimer's. Now one sees
a title like *Elephants Can Remember* as an explanation

buried in your *three-fold increase in indefinite nouns, eighteen percent
increase in phrase repetition, and thirty percent decline in vocabulary.*

Readers simply thought the plot confusing
and the characters lacking in . . . character.

Eighty years old, a broken hip,
who knows how many medications.

The current hypothesis is that you were your forgetful
heroine-turned-non who could no longer solve the mystery.

You became Ariadne and she, you. Old girl,
have you any appreciation of the poignancy?

Decades later computer linguists mark a significant
turn—*indefinite decline*—in your seventy-third book, confirming

readers' reactions. And then you kept on writing? All
the way up to eighty books? Protected by family, did you know you

were soldiering on? What was that like? Oh, forget
that. I'm not sure we would want to know, even if we could.

Verdi Would Have Wept

Florence Foster Jenkins just sang and died.

But not before marrying into syphilis,
spending her father's fortune on New York's elite,
taking opera lessons from unknown

teachers. She was known for singing off key.

After countless private performances,
tableaux-vivants,
breakfasts and balls,
she booked Carnegie Hall
October 25, 1944.

Cole Porter, Gian Carlo Menotti, and others attended.
The audience applauded, whistled
to cover their laughter.
Handkerchiefs stifled the chortling.
Aisle-sitters could leave
if it became too much.
Florence professed the laughter
she did hear
came from
hoodlums planted in the audience
by her enemies.

Newspaper reviews? Neutral to
cruel. *She has a great voice. In fact,
she can sing anything but notes.*
St. Clair Bayfield, her manager of 36 years:
She had not known, you see.

Five days later,
while shopping at Schirmer's Music,
Florence's heart stopped.
A month later,
she died, known

to have said,
People may say I can't sing,
but
no one
can ever say I didn't sing.

mom's cast-iron skillet

along with her chipped, black-handled pancake turner
accompanies me to campsite #53, Pocahontas State Park,

sits on a degraded grey wooden picnic table, soots up
on campfire's grate, offers fluffy yellow eggs, bacon, veggies.

my hand wobbles: how did she even hold a cast-iron skillet
long enough to feed us, raise a daughter full of sparks dying

on their way to the heavens? What tension is born of heat and flight!
mother gone, daughter remains, happy to use her utensils—

there is more to heaviness and soot than I'd realized.

Family Traumas

All of us cart them around,
weeping and wailing,
lugging their unbearable weight,
or folding them into a napkin, discreetly
sliding them into our back pockets.

Mine is my mother's fear of illness.
Her mother died of breast cancer—
lymphatic arm amputated—
no fun for the sixteen-year-old bon vivant
driving friends to milkshakes and cherry cokes in her convertible.
Nor for her twin sister caring for their ailing mother.
Going to the hospital is the hardest work in the world,
my mother always said.

That is why, when I had my own cancer,
I could not let her come and take care of me.
She did not know how to take care of and I did not
know how to be cared for.
There was too much weeping and wailing
stuffed into our back pockets.

It's Time for a Cat

Her immune system, infused with the cocktail
Adriamycin *(the red devil)* and Cytoxan,
fought infection's red, thrush's white.

Household surfaces bleached, baldness
swathed, she lived pet-less until
the worst of the assault had passed.

Treatment completed, she thought,
It's time for a cat! Talk of a new normal only makes
sense when the old curls up and falls asleep on her lap.

Educating Rachael

Young. Brilliant. She doesn't know of Baryshnikov,
The Rain in Spain, or how to talk to a stranger.

Sound white-wires to her brain 24/7.
I yearn to sing her of the plain in Spain,

show her Mikhail defying gravity, ascending
to heaven, me in tow.

I want her to lose the ear buds, engage the moment.
Instead I sink into my own; where is the heat here?

What do I want for her? To taste paradise, drink deeply of love,
trust her voice, and treasure her creations.

I want this to happen, yet fear it may not.

Little Lincoln

I haven't slept well.
The red neon sign at the breakfast dive blinks
Open. 6:50 a.m. The coffee's hot.

I shake the dust off my dreams; politics continue
to haunt. Stephen Colbert made me laugh,
tucked me in, then left me to my nightmares.

I ask my server how her pregnant co-worker is.
My sister? You mean the girl with the tattoos down her other arm?
My waitress's right arm, fully tatted, motions toward her plain left.

She's your sister? I didn't know that!
Yeah, she had the baby in August, calls him Lincoln.
Where'd she get the name Lincoln?

I think it's from Abraham Lincoln—she's a big history buff, reads a lot.
His middle name is Alyosha, or something like that. Can't pronounce it.
Her husband's from Iran. But I get to babysit and hold him on Sunday!

I sigh. If this young woman, working for minimum wage in a diner, one semester short of a bachelor's degree, with her Iranian husband and several kids in tow, names her newborn Lincoln Alyosha (or something like that) then all

will be well.

after dessert

yesterday
Hannah died.
twenty-two years old.
countless pills.

her Grandmother took the call
between appetizers and entrée.

after dessert, we found out.

dining table turned to altar.
herbal tea, tissues, and tears.
we lived the pain of loss,
had only each other
in this now-sacred space.

When My Mother Met the Queen

Every woman is a queen—secretly, of course.
A walk at Balmoral with corgis at your feet.
Goodness, by virtue of what it is, shares itself.

My mother perceived herself as serf to the queen.
A '50s bayside town, kids surfing at her feet.
Every woman is a queen, secretly, of course.

Fanfares hushed by whining children yearning to swim.
Democracy's small towns; danger takes a back seat.
Goodness, by virtue of what it is, shares itself.

Baby oil, suburb death, loneliness unseen.
The omega to alpha royalty's replete.
Every woman is a queen, secretly, of course.

Royalty pays a price for privileges unseen.
Bestowing worth, the lone figurehead dares to lead.
Goodness, by virtue of what it is, shares itself.

The meeting, the handshake, and the locked gaze between,
Allowed my mother to know we all are complete.
Every woman is a queen, secretly, of course.
Goodness, by virtue of what it is, shares itself.

Four Poems on Camille Claudel

The Devil's Basket

1.

Red clay: soft, deep within my hands,
squishy, gooey, responsive to my touch.

At the bottom of the ditch, in after-dinner dark, I dig.
Clay, clay, more clay! My pail fills. I water

the clay for the night, place a cloth over the top.
I have made myself a glorious tomorrow.

2.

My secret friend, clay, listens, follows my forming,
leans into me. It is not like mother who never hugs,

or Paul, or her favorite, Louise. It is not like the art teacher
at the Catholic school down the road showing off

my twelve-year-old self's drawings, unaware of my sculptures,
my David and Goliath, much admired when I was thirteen.

3.

Mother never kisses us, we quarrel. Grandpa's kiln fires clay into roof tiles.
Monsieur Colin homeschools Latin, reads us "Oedipus" and "Antigone."

Paul and I escape to the Devil's Basket's caves, ride serpents' backs,
roam with the rock creatures as the rugged terrain shapes us.

We, in turn, will shape it.
Paul with words. I, form.

Too Many Ideas

In the 1880s France blossomed paintings,
birthed form from earth, celebrated
color, light, and shadow. Redon painted
flowers of dreams, fauna of the imagination.

The Salon in Paris honored traditionalists, ate
its young. Accused of sculpting from cast—not
models or photos—Rodin established innocence
by sculpting larger than life.

Camille Claudel, acclaimed sculptor and Rodin's lover,
was accused of using his drawings. Her response:
*I never draw inspiration from anyone other
than myself, having too many ideas rather than too few.*

Camille, your whirlwind of ideas and inspiration left you
feverishly unable to keep up with the sculptor's loop.
You witnessed connections that faded like old photos,
yet continued to fuel yourself with the currents of the ages!

Bravo! Living for a moment in a glorious flow
you knew all too well was not yours, you
were magically transported to the heavens, then
returned, oh so gently, back to this earth.

Camille Bicycles through Paris, Spring 1887

Cobblestone-clatter.
Swinging their legs
over the bar, pantalooned
women grasp the handlebars,
look left, right, ride.

French braid un-
braided. Something is
unraveling, attempting
to reveal itself. She likes
this. Clay and castings

drain her budget,
feet, arms. Marble releases—
reluctantly—its creations.
No matter, she rides.
Silt- and sand-dusted,

she cannot draw
the nude, but can be
Rodin's lover, student. She
thrusts her leg over the bar,
bicycles topless through Paris.

We have no proof
Camille Claudel did this,
but note her saucy responses
written in an album
at the home of Florence Jean,
her friend on the Isle of Wight:

Your favorite virtue:
I don't have any: they are all boring.
Your favorite qualities in a man:
To obey his wife.
Your favorite qualities in a woman:
To make her husband fret.

Your favorite poet:
One who does not write verses.

I Take My Hammer

> *When something unpleasant happens to me, I take my hammer and I squash a figure . . . a pile of rubble accumulates in the middle of my atelier, it is a real human sacrifice.*
> ~Camille Claudel, Letter to Henriette Thierry,
> December 1912

Furious, sad, unable to escape distress weighing more
than marble itself, I throw my wax models into the fire.
They flame. Wild light dances the walls, warms
my feet this dreary December day.

Beloved Henri, mon cousin, has died.
When something unpleasant happens
I take the hammer to my works. He knew me.
You, oh Mother, Paul, and Louise, do not.

Inspiration wanes. Illness and the executions
continue until the rubble becomes its own
sad creation—worthy of any sculptor—
in the middle of my atelier's floor.

I cannot shake this, Henri. I did not expect
to co-create with despair, can bear this
weight no longer. I have no resources, eat little,
create even less, worry so much more.

I Know How

to do this, if
you want to. Resist
today, embrace
tomorrow when I'll be
on duty.
I know how to
stop his suffering,
render death natural as
IVs, beeps, and
flashing numbers
fall to the floor and slink
out of the room.
Watching, waiting, willing has
taken its toll. Hope
landed on eyelid's flutter,
squeezed your hand;
you believed it.
*I know how
to do this.* He
will breathe
for a while, eventually
stop.
It is usually peaceful. Painless.
I know how to do this;
I know you don't.

Keeping Count

1.

12:37 EDT, October 2, 2017.
WCVE at 88.9 on the dial pre-empts
normal programming.
Radio and smart phone on my lap concur.
58 dead—higher than the 49 at Pulse—
and potentially rising as the day weeps on.

2.

64-year-old Stephen, 32 floors above the crowd,
grabs 23 firearms stored in 10 suitcases.
Country music wails, beer cans hiss,
the Route 91 Harvest Music Fest explodes.

3.

I've been here 66 years, 243 days, and 12 hours.
Regularly check *Richmond Times-Dispatch* obits.
Lived longer than many, not as long as some.

4.

One memory. Driving home from the beach we stop
at the mangled cars. Pulled from the wreckage,
a man screeches as the bone protruding
from his right arm catches on the van door.
I hold another's hand, whispering hope. The rest
of the drive home, I count:
5 billboards. 4 turning cars.
3 oak trees. 2 eyes. Countless tears.
I sink farther into and out of myself.
1, 2, 3, 4, 5, 6, 7, 8.
Self-care comes in all shapes and sizes.

5.

58 dead.
489 injured.
10 suitcases.

Making of an Enemy

> *~after Randall Jarrell's "The Death of the Ball Turret Gunner"*

From border's legal crossing I fell into the State
And nurtured a rape child in my belly.
Fourteen years old, separated from my parents,
Dates of assault, menstrual cycle tracked,
Caged, and baby birthed, I became State's enemy;
And you wonder why.

Metallic Transfer Cases

Coffins, warehoused abroad,
return soldiers to our homeland via Dover
Air Force Base.

His family dreads seeing the ramp descend
from the back of the transport jet,
yet it does.

Six soldiers, white gloved, camouflaged in desert garb,
carry him down, line him up in a sea of red, white, and blue
in the shelter.

Surrounded by silver—hangar, mortuary instruments, steps, and stars—
he is welcomed home, while all
of the color in his family's life turns to grey.

The End of This

> *A few months ago, I used this candle for a vigil for a young man who was murdered on the streets of East Baltimore. And here I am again . . .*
> ~woman mourning the death of Freddie Gray, Baltimore, April 2015

The match flames
blue as I light
the ten-inch taper,
white-wicked, not a dent, not
a scar. I whisper
a prayer for Freddie.
We cannot get to the end
of this candle.

Black Lives Matter,
so I relight my burnt
candle, march, sing.
It isn't white or
black that concern
me. It's blue. Baton Rouge—
months, vigils
later—I relight my candle's
black wick. Its light
does not soothe; its wax
wounds.

Mothers of the Movement
squint in TV lights,
demand justice. Suited
police commissioners
apologize, create
task forces to mitigate
their tasks of force.

We cannot get to the end of this candle.

Downsizing

The shredder is broken,
too much crammed in.
I feed the other one and break it too.

Bank statements, old love letters,
report cards released from yellowed boxes and
browned newspapers from 1978.

The boxes implore me to discard a get-well card, keep the
playbill with me as Gypsy's bump-it-with-a-trumpet girl.
They flap tan arms. *Over here! Over here!*

Over here? When did you learn to speak, you boxes?
I snuggle the best memories into them.
Tape straps them in; they patiently wait for my next visit.

At some point the boxes will beckon me. *Invite us to a party!*
Let us reveal you to you! Champagne! A toast!
The party is wonderful. *You boxes, you knew all along!*

The Gesture

Three friends at restaurant's table lean into each other.
The room hard, sharp; sound ricochets off ceilings and walls.

One drives. One can't see at night. The third doesn't drive—neurologist's orders.
Aging poorly, slowed speech, slower thought, the effort lives on her face.

She touches my left hand—gold and diamonds—knows how precious this is.
What does she remember of my wedding six months prior? What is with her still?

I joke. If I forget to wear my rings, I hear about it. Cute, but not true.
Laughter shields us from this brutal aging. Loss stares us directly in the eye.

I long for the present that just flew by on the wings of a stupid joke.
My friend was here in that moment; I don't know how many more we'll have.

Bus Stop to Nowhere

Forgetting

>why she came to the iron-benched, green and yellow government bus stop in Dusseldorf, Germany, her calming

is

>real, although the bus stop is not. It was built next to the home for the aged to contain this demented wanderer and

both

>the panicked intrusion of troubling memories and her present peace.

the

>nurse sits with her, holding hands, offering a cup of tea upon return to the home as the

problem

>magically resolves before their eyes, reality shifting from past to present

and

>given time, the distress resolves of its own accord. It is

the

>gift of wise, compassionate caregivers—this bus stop to nowhere— that honors the intricacies of memory, problem, and

solution.

Eleanor, Speak

Eleanor, speak to us right
here, right now. You were the reluctant
president's wife, public speaker, symbol, saint.

You bravely hoisted yourself out of depression,
vaulted above your introversion, and
landed squarely in fairness and justice.

You've seen it all: a world in two wars,
a wounded serviceman here, statesman there,
an aftermath in which you've created peace,

co-written charters, chapters of *My Day*,
resisted for race's sake,
replaced hatred with justice and love.

Eleanor, speak to us right
here, right now. What would Donald
weigh on the scales of justice?

Eleanor, what would you do?
Join an Indivisible group, give to the ACLU,
write letters-to-the-editor,

wear a pussy hat, pen a poem? How would you be?
Anxious? Afraid? Wind knocked out
of your sails? Or thinking, *"Same old, same old?"*

Eleanor, speak.

Notre Dame

> *A major fire has engulfed the medieval cathedral of Notre-Dame in Paris. The 850-year-old Gothic building's spire and roof have collapsed, but the main structure, including the two bell towers, has been saved.*
> *~BBC News, April 19, 2019*

Oh, Lady, today
we weep for you.

Gobsmacked at your collapsing
spire, glorious rose windows, sonorous
pipes and bells,
all in peril.

No organ's seven-second ring
when the ceiling cradling its sound
has crumbled. Do pictures of Christ
still line the nave?

Thirty years ago, red-eye flight,
Charles DeGaulle. Six a.m. I forced
wakefulness, walked zombie-like
through the streets of Paris.

There you were! Stone carvings of the Virgin, St. Anne,
and the Last Judgment arched above your front portals.
Rib-vaulted ceilings, bathed in light high
as heaven itself, lifted and grounded me.

I lit a votive, prayed. My sleepy head drooped
above the candles. A voice from fifty years ago:
Be careful: don't lean too close. Sister Grace, with me still.
You'll catch your hair on fire!

Notes

"The Seventy-Third Book: Letter to Agatha Christie" refers to facts about Agatha Christie (September 15, 1890–January 12, 1976) that I learned from the public radio show *Radiolab*. Ariadne was a princess in Greek mythology associated with mazes and labyrinths. Agatha Christie is an everyday heroine.

"Verdi Would Have Wept" describes the deliciously complex story of Florence Foster Jenkins (July 19, 1868–November 26, 1944). Was she a fool or heroine of her own life? Some of her performances can be found on YouTube.

"mom's cast-iron skillet" reflects my astonishment at the emotions evoked by the possessions of lost loved ones. Pocahontas State Park is near Richmond, Virginia.

"Family Traumas" explores the generational nature of trauma. It is about trauma transmitted through a combination of environment, genetics, and archetype operating oftentimes below the surface of awareness, yet having a tremendous effect on future generations.

"It's Time for a Cat" describes my journey through breast cancer treatment. I tired of the "new normal" phrase. Yet with the return of a missed and comforting "normal" in my life, I finally understood.

"Educating Rachael" describes my hopes for younger generations and fears they may not attain what is so precious to me. In 2015 the Pew Research Center noted that 92 percent of teens surveyed in the United States reported going online daily, with 24 percent saying they go online "almost constantly" (*https://www.pewresearch.org/internet/2015/04/09/teens-social-media-technology-2015*). This cannot help but have consequences for mental and physical health, social skills, privacy, and life itself.

"Little Lincoln" comes from a true story. It is dedicated to my server at McLean's Restaurant, my "breakfast office," in Richmond, Virginia.

"after dessert" refers to the surprising and tragic death of Hannah. The

Centers for Disease Control and Prevention (CDC) reported that, in 2018, suicide was the second leading cause of death among individuals between the ages of 10 and 34. It was the tenth leading cause of death overall in the United States, claiming the lives of more than 48,000 people. (*https://www.nimh.nih.gov/health/statistics/suicide.shtml*).

"When My Mother Met the Queen" is dedicated to 1950s and '60s housewives who lived the American dream, yet felt something missing. They often drew importance and referred glory from royalty and movie stars. It is written in villanelle form.

The next four poems are about Camille Claudel, renowned French sculptor born on December 8, 1864. Her story encompasses everything from the joy and genius of creation to her battles with her family, the French arts community, and her lover Auguste Rodin, and her 30-year incarceration in a mental asylum until the end of her life. In 2017, the Musée Camille Claudel opened at 10 Rue Gustave Flaubert, 10400 Nogent-sur-Seine, outside of Paris.

"The Devil's Basket" is the site where Camille and her younger brother Paul Claudel—French poet, dramatist, and diplomat—enjoyed many a summer day playing on rocks shaped like animals and mythological creatures. This landscape influenced both Paul as a playwright and Camille as a sculptor.

"Too Many Ideas" is what Camille claimed when accused of appropriating Rodin's ideas during the decade they worked together. As he gained greater fame, her genius also began to be recognized. She became known for her sculptures La Valse, Clotho, and Les Causeuses. This poem is an homage to creativity.

"Camille Bicycles through Paris, Spring 1887" has Camille living and working in Paris after her family relocated to the Montparnasse area in 1881. Women slowly began to engage in the latest fad of bicycling. In 1892, the Minister of the Interior stated, "The wear of masculine clothes by women is tolerated only for the purpose of Velocipedic sport." Bicycling women appeared to challenge the culture on many different levels. Camille did as well. She enrolled in The Academie Colarossi where women could gain entrance, study, and draw the nude. She rented an atelier with other young female sculptors, studied under Alfred Boucher, and modeled and studied with Auguste Rodin.

"I Take My Hammer" describes the first part of Camille's descent into illness. The quote upon which this poem is based is contained in a letter to Henriette Thierry, December 1912 (private collection, in *L'Oeuvre de Camille Claudel*, p. 271). Camille ended her nearly ten-year love affair with Rodin, continuing to see him occasionally in social situations and receiving financial support from him. She grew to distrust Rodin, lived by herself in a studio/apartment in Paris, and became increasingly isolated and ill. In 1913, against the advice of the asylum's medical director, her brother Paul Claudel signed her commitment papers. She lived out the remaining thirty years of her life at Asile de Montdevergues, an asylum outside of Avignon. She died in 1943. I highly recommend *Camille Claudel: A Life* (Harry M. Abrams, New York, 2002) by Odile Ayral-Clause to those interested in learning more about Camille.

"I Know How" is dedicated to a nurse at Brigham and Women's Hospital in Boston, Massachusetts. This is one way in which she helped our family decide to remove my critically ill brother from the ventilator. Head swathed in a turban, she was going through her own chemotherapy. After chemo, stem cell transplants, and the like had ceased to work for my brother, we made the decision. She was a godsend.

"Keeping Count" is dedicated to those injured and killed in the mass shooting in Las Vegas, Nevada, in 2017. Researchers have difficulty agreeing upon a definition for "mass shooting," resulting in a lack of data concerning these types of murders. What we do know is that active shooters account for a small percentage of gun-related deaths (*https://www.pewresearch.org/fact-tank/2019/08/16/what-the-data-says-about-gun-deaths-in-the-u-s/*). I would posit, however, that they significantly affect our use of public spaces through the fear they generate.

"Making of an Enemy" is modeled after Randall Jarrell's "The Death of the Ball Turret Gunner," one of the most powerful anti-war poems of the WWII era. In his war against immigrants and asylum seekers, former President Trump's head of the Office of Refugee Resettlement (ORR), Scott Lloyd, kept a spreadsheet of information on pregnant minors in his care, including dates of their periods and whether any minors had asked for an abortion. Teens in ORR custody, many of whom faced a high risk of rape and sexual assault during their journey to the U.S., were required to get the director's approval before terminating a pregnancy.

"Metallic Transfer Cases" describes the grief of those who have lost loved ones in military action. A related note: the Dover Ban (referring to Dover Air Force Base) was instituted from 1991 to 2009. It is a policy that forbids the press from taking photographs when remains of deceased public soldiers travel to and from the U.S. (*https://lawjournal.ku.edu/wp-content/uploads/2020/08/Kelley-V26I1.pdf*).

"The End of This" is a quote from a woman reflecting upon the 2014 killing of Michael Brown in Ferguson, Missouri. "Black men and boys face the highest risk of being killed by police—at a rate of 96 out of 100,000 deaths. By comparison, white men and boys face a lower rate of 39 per 100,000 deaths, despite being a bigger portion of the U.S. population. Overall, men faced a rate of 52 per 100,000 deaths" (*https://www.pbs.org/newshour/health/after-ferguson-black-men-and-boys-still-face-the-highest-risk-of-being-killed-by-police*).

"Downsizing" is a crazy act, a blend of sweet reminiscence, embarrassment, and unforgotten and too-much-remembered moments. Those who don't downsize are welcome to engage one of the booming industries in America today: self-storage units. A 10-by-10-foot unit typically runs about $100 a month.

"The Gesture" is dedicated to my mentor and friend, Lynn Barnett.

"Bus Stop to Nowhere" comes from a story I heard on public radio's *Radiolab*. I often tease about "that German engineering," something

I think is okay since I have a German background. In this instance I was taken by this project's beautiful blend of common sense and compassion.

"Eleanor, Speak" alludes to my admiration for Eleanor Roosevelt (October 11, 1884–November 7, 1962). She served as the First Lady of the United States from March 4, 1933, to April 12, 1945, and as the United States Delegate to the United Nations General Assembly from 1945 to 1952. In that capacity she helped to write the Universal Declaration of Human Rights. She hosted news conferences, wrote daily newspaper columns, and advocated for human rights. In today's political climate I sometimes wish I could speak to her. I have no doubt that she would have something to say, something to do, and share her passion about our America.

"Notre Dame" is an homage to the cathedral and my Catholic upbringing. It is also a tribute to one of the most beautiful and historic buildings in the world. I cried that day.

Nan Ottenritter is a poet and musician working and living in Richmond, Virginia. She was born and raised in Baltimore, Maryland, and obtained degrees from Frostburg State College, Johns Hopkins University, and Howard University. She spent her career in the community college world, first teaching at Hagerstown Junior College, where she was awarded Teacher of the Year. Nan managed national projects for the American Association of Community Colleges and ended her formal career by serving as the director of professional development for the Virginia Community College System.

Nan is a fiddler in the Appalachian tradition, a bicyclist, traveler, lover of the written and spoken word, and, most recently, a rejuvenated American citizen involved in civic life through political action and writing about our cultural and political zeitgeist.

Her works have appeared in *TheNewVerse.News, North of Oxford, Artemis Journals: Women hold up half the sky* (2018 and 2019 editions), *Poets Reading the News, Life in 10 Minutes, Anthology of the Poetry Society of Virginia (2019),* and *As You Were: The Military Review.* She is a member of the Poetry Society of Virginia and enjoys giving readings, teaching, and participating in the rich poetry community of Richmond.

Her current writing projects include a book about her experiences in the Covid-19 pandemic, a work about French sculptor Camille Claudel, and a collection of poems based on her father's WWII experience. Nan resides in Richmond with her wife, two cats, and several raised beds of vegetables—all of which provided great company and comfort during the pandemic.

www.ingramcontent.com/pod-product-compliance
Lightning Source LLC
LaVergne TN
LVHW041600070426
835507LV00011B/1216